Martin Luther King Jr.

FERGUSON
CAREER BIOGRAPHIES

Martin Luther King Jr.

Minister and Civil Rights Activist

BRENDAN JANUARY

Ferguson Publishing Company
Chicago, Illinois

Photographs ©: AP/Wideworld: 12, 20, 25 52, Perry Aycock 55, 60, 64, 71, 84, 91, 94; Archive: 29, 66, 80, 81, 87, 96, 105; Corbis: 8, 38, 40, 43, 49, 77, 79, 89, 98, 108; Liaison: 57, 106.

An Editorial Directions Book

Library of Congress Cataloging-in-Publication Data
January, Brendan, 1972–
     Martin Luther King, Jr. : minister and civil rights leader / by Brendan January.
     p. cm. — (Ferguson's career biographies)
     Includes bibliographical references and index.
     ISBN 0-89434-342-4
     1.King, Martin Luther, Jr., 1929–1968—Juvenile literature. 2. Afro-Americans—Biography—Juvenile literature. 3. Civil rights workers—United States—Biography—Juvenile literature. 4. Baptists—United States—Clergy—Biography—Juvenile literature. 5. Afro-Americans—Civil rights—History—20th century—Juvenile literature. [1. King, Martin Luther, Jr., 1929–1968. 2. Civil rights workers. 3. Clergy. 4. Afro-Americans—Biography.]
I. Title. II. Series.

E185.97.K5 J36 2000
323'092—dc21
[B]
                                                         00-037618

Copyright © 2000 by Ferguson Publishing Company
Published and distributed by
Ferguson Publishing Company
200 West Jackson Boulevard, Suite 700
Chicago, Illinois 60606
www.fergpubco.com

Printed in the United States of America
X-8

CONTENTS

Martin Luther King Jr.

Atlanta in 1930. Martin Luther King Jr. was born into a racist environment in the segregated South.

GROWING UP IN SEGREGATION

MARTIN LUTHER KING JR. was born in Atlanta on January 15, 1929. As an adult, Martin would move millions of people with his words. But as a newborn baby, he was so quiet that the doctor feared he was stillborn.

Martin's father was Michael King, the pastor of Ebenezer Baptist Church in Atlanta. As a minister of a large congregation, King Sr. became an important leader of Atlanta's black community. He grew wealthy from his business dealings and bought a large house for his family.

On Sundays, young Martin would watch his father mount the pulpit in front of the packed church and preach for hours. After the services, Martin went to Sunday school, where teachers vividly told him the stories, lessons, and characters of the Bible. By the age of five, Martin could recite complex biblical passages from memory.

Segregation in the South

Before Martin entered school, his favorite playmate was a white boy. In September 1935, both boys started school, but Martin quickly noticed that his friend went to one school, and he went to another.

Shortly after class began, the white boy told Martin that they could no longer play together. Stunned, Martin asked why. "Because we are white and you are colored," he explained.

Confused and hurt by the answer, Martin told his parents what the white boy had said. Martin's parents began telling Martin, then only six years old, about slavery and the devastating racism that crushed black people after the Civil War. They told him how whites maintained their superiority across the country, and especially in the South, through violence and segregation.

Segregation ruled the South. Hundreds of thousands of blacks and whites lived and worked side by side in Atlanta, but custom and laws kept them separate, a pattern repeated in nearly every southern town not only in Georgia but in all southern states.

But segregation did more than just separate the races. It created the impression that the white race was superior and that the black race was inferior. In waiting rooms, at lunch counters, in rest rooms, even at drinking fountains, blacks saw signs that read WHITES ONLY. Everyday, in a thousand different ways, blacks were reminded that they were inferior, excluded, not human. Some whites justified segregation by saying that each race enjoyed separate but equal facilities.

But separate did not mean equal. Whites sat in clean train cars while blacks huddled in filthy boxcars normally used to carry animals. Whites sat in sturdy seats in the clean section of the movie theater while blacks used a separate entrance to sit in the balcony. Whites went to modern schools while blacks struggled to learn in buildings with broken windows and old textbooks. Segregation spread bitterness, crushed dreams, and dashed the bright hopes of black youth.

The Ku Klux Klan

Those who tried to break through the walls of segregation faced the wrath of the Ku Klux Klan (KKK). The KKK was an organization formed after the Civil War which thrived in the former Confederate states. They were dedicated to maintaining white superiority at all costs, and members of the KKK terrorized blacks who tried to assert their rights. Blacks who were convicted of crimes by all-white juries were often dragged from their jail cells by mobs and hung from a tree.

No justice. A black man in the South is beaten and murdered before he can stand trial.

Almost all whites believed in white superiority—city leaders, business leaders, preachers, the police, judges, teachers, factory workers. Tragically, many blacks believed it too.

"You must never feel that you are less than someone else," Martin's mother urged him. "You must always feel that you are somebody."

Martin didn't feel inferior to anyone. In his family and in Atlanta's black community, Martin was encouraged to develop his talents. He also learned at an early age that you could fight segregation.

When Martin was still a boy, his father took him to a shoe store in downtown Atlanta. They sat in seats at the front and waited for service. A young white clerk saw them and came over.

"I'll be happy to wait on you if you'll just move to those seats in the rear," he said.

Martin's father didn't move. "There's nothing wrong with these seats. We're quite comfortable here," he answered.

"Sorry, but you'll have to move," said the clerk.

"We'll either buy shoes sitting here," said Martin's father, "or we won't buy shoes at all."

The conversation ended there. Martin's father grabbed Martin's hand and marched out of the store.

"I don't care how long I have to live with this system," he told Martin. "I will never accept it."

Martin later wrote in *Stride toward Freedom* that he never seen his father more angry.

Martin's father drove a car instead of riding the trains or buses. He would not allow himself to be humiliated by sitting or standing in a "colored" section. Once, King Sr. and Martin were driving when a policeman suddenly appeared and ordered them to pull over.

"Boy, show me your license," said the police officer to Martin's father.

"Do you see this child here?" he shot back, pointing to Martin sitting next to him. "That's a boy there. I'm a man. I'm Reverend King."

The policeman had been used to hearing blacks mumble agreement to his orders. But King Sr.'s sharp reply left him so shaken that he jumped back onto his motorcycle and sped off.

Martin wrote later, again in *Stride toward Freedom*: "I could never adjust to the separate waiting rooms, separate eating places, separate rest rooms, partly because the separate was always unequal, and partly because the very idea of separation did something to my sense of dignity and self respect."

Still, everywhere Martin went, he read the WHITES ONLY sign. He saw it at swimming pools, in parks, in restaurants, at the theater. He grew angry and resentful of a world that told him he was inferior and less than human.

Martin became a scrappy fighter and someone who played basketball, football, and baseball with a ruthless, competitive spirit. In school, Martin skipped grades with little effort.

By the time he was a teenager, Martin had grown into a dark-skinned young man with almond-shaped eyes and a smooth, rich baritone voice. King Sr. wanted Martin to become a preacher and eventually take over his pulpit.

Martin did have talent as a speaker. At home, he practiced his speech techniques in front of a mirror and won first prize in a speech competition in high school. But Martin resisted his father. He felt that religion was too much yelling, clapping, and singing, with not enough solving the world's problems of poverty, racism, and disease.

Instead, at the age of fifteen, Martin entered Morehouse College, a black college in Atlanta. There, he encountered professors who pressed him to develop his vocabulary and speaking skills. They urged him to find solutions to the injustices. Martin pondered the problem. How could he destroy segregation in a land ruled by whites?

Martin felt the need to help blacks escape the horrors of segregation. He considered becoming a doctor, a lawyer, a teacher. But at Morehouse, he met a minister who preached both the word of God and social protest. Martin realized that leading a church could allow him to be a force for change.

Martin decided to become a preacher after all. On February 25, 1948, he was ordained and became an assistant pastor to his father at Ebenezer. But Martin wanted more education. In 1948, he entered Crozer Theological Seminary in Chester, Pennsylvania, one of the best seminaries in the country.

"You're awfully young to go to Crozer," his father huffed.

But Martin's mind was made up. He packed his bags and left his southern home. For the first time in his life, he studied in a school with mostly white students. Surrounded by different people and new ideas at Crozer, Martin experienced a stunning period of intellectual and personal growth. Most important, he learned the philosophies he would later use to launch the civil rights movement.

STUDIES

2

MARTIN FELT INTIMIDATED when he first stepped onto the campus at Crozer. Surrounded by almost one hundred white students, he constantly felt the need to prove himself. He studied long into the night, kept himself immaculately clean, and always arrived at class on time.

Martin read the great philosophers— Plato, Aristotle, Rousseau, Hobbes, Locke. But an unforgettable lecture changed his life. King went to Philadelphia to hear Dr. Mordecai W. Johnson describe his stay in

India with Mahatma Gandhi. The British had ruled India for more than 150 years, when Gandhi launched a revolution that broke Britain's power and won India's independence. But King was fascinated by how Gandhi had used nonviolence to achieve victory. Instead of leading rebels with guns, Gandhi had organized massive demonstrations with no violence to resist British control. The British could have easily crushed an armed rebellion. But millions of Indians used boycotts and strikes, and the mighty British Empire was forced to withdraw from the Indian subcontinent.

Gandhi preached that love, not hate, was the weapon to use against injustice.

King could hardly contain his excitement. At last, he had found a philosophy that could change the world for the better.

King graduated from Crozer in May 1951 at the top of his class. He applied to and was accepted at Boston University, where he worked for a doctorate in theology. In February 1952, King met a lovely young woman named Coretta Scott. After one date, King found her intelligent, beautiful, and irresistible. Within a year, he had convinced her to marry him.

A Dilemma

In August 1953, King faced a dilemma. He had completed his courses for his doctoral degree and needed only to write his dissertation. He could pursue several options for the next year. Three colleges had offered him posts—one as a professor, one as a dean, and the last as an administrator. Two churches—one in Massachusetts, the other in New York—were interested in calling him to preach in their pulpits.

While King wrestled with these options, he received a letter from the Dexter Avenue Baptist Church in Montgomery, Alabama. They invited him to preach there.

The church intrigued King. The size of the congregation was only three hundred, but the members were the leaders and professionals of the city's black community. The church also had an outstanding reputation for its well-trained and educated preachers. King replied that he would be in Atlanta for the Christmas holidays and would be happy to preach then.

For his tryout, King gave a sermon titled "The Three Dimensions of a Complete Life." When he left, King did not know how the congregation

Where the work began. Martin Luther King Jr. served as pastor of the Dexter Avenue Baptist Church in Montgomery.

received his preaching. But a month after he had returned to Boston, King received a special letter delivered by airmail. The church invited him to be their pastor.

The news delighted King, but he was still torn. Could he return to the South?

He hated segregation, the humiliation of drinking from separate fountains, riding in the back of the bus, sitting in separate, filthy seats in the movie theater. He wondered if he could subject his wife to it. In the North, they had grown used to more freedom, even though the line between the races was often drawn as strictly as it was in the South.

And what about their children? Would they escape the humiliation of segregation?

A Return to the South

Still, King realized that the South was his home, and he loved it despite the evil of racism. In April 1954, King accepted the post. As King prepared to give his first sermons, events occurred in the nation that would act as an earthquake to the social structure in the South.

In May 1954, the U.S. Supreme Court ruled in *Brown v. Board of Education* that segregation in schools was unconstitutional.

As news of the decision spread, white southerners gasped with baffled rage. "There won't be any integration in Mississippi," vowed one. "Not now, not 100 years from now, maybe not 6,000 years from now—maybe never."

BOYCOTT

KING WAS THRILLED by the Court's decision, but he had little time to enjoy it. Church duties kept him occupied from morning till night. King became a great speaker, able to move his congregation to heights of joy with his emotional and intelligent sermons. He became active in the National Association for the Advancement of Colored People (NAACP), an organization that had been fighting for black rights since 1909. He also launched social programs to help sick parishioners and help pay scholarships for blacks hoping to study in college.

King met another young preacher named Ralph Abernathy, who preached at nearby First Baptist Church. King and Abernathy became fast friends and discussed ways to mobilize Montgomery's black community for social change. But racism lay at the heart of the city's social order. Montgomery was the first capital of the Confederate States of America. The city's 90,000 whites expected the 50,000 blacks to stay out of politics and city life. To King's disappointment, most of them did.

Life in Montgomery

King settled into life in Montgomery. He earned his doctorate in spring 1955, and Coretta became pregnant. Then, on December 2, 1955, King received a phone call that would change his life. He learned that a black woman named Rosa Parks had been arrested for refusing to give up her bus seat for a white passenger.

The city's buses had always been strictly segregated. Whites sat in the front and blacks sat in the back. If the white section filled up, the blacks seated in the next row had to vacate their spaces for a white passenger. Blacks were not allowed to walk through the white section. After they paid their fare at the front, black passengers were forced to step back outside, walk along the side of the bus, and enter through the rear door. In a cruel joke, the white bus driver would sometimes speed off before the black passenger had made it to the rear door, leaving the passenger without a fare and standing in a cloud of exhaust. The steady stream of humiliations and slights created a smoldering rage within the black community.

A Brave Woman on a Bus

On December 1, 1955, forty-three-year-old Rosa Parks had boarded a bus to go home. Parks sat in a seat just behind the white section. The bus soon filled with passengers until no seats were left. When another white passenger boarded, the bus driver turned and told the four blacks to leave their seats and stand in the rear. When they didn't move, the driver stood up.

"Y'all make it light on yourself and let me have those seats," he shouted. Three of them quickly stood and shuffled to the rear of the bus.

Parks, however, remained seated. After a day of work and shopping, her feet throbbed with pain. The driver stood over her and threatened to call the police.

A brave woman. After she refused to give up her bus seat for a white passenger, Rosa Parks was arrested and fined.

"You may do that," she replied, her voice barely rising above a whisper. She wasn't moving. Two patrolmen arrived and took her to the downtown police station, where she was fingerprinted and locked in jail.

Edgar D. Nixon, a railroad porter who also the head of the local NAACP, was shocked when he learned that Parks had been arrested. Parks was well known and respected in the black community. He rushed to the jail and paid the three hundred dollar bail to have her released. That evening, Nixon asked Parks if he could use her case to challenge the segregation laws in court. Parks consulted with her family and agreed.

The next morning, Nixon called King.

"We have took this type of thing too long already," he said, "We got to boycott the buses. . . . Make it clear to the white folks we ain't taking this type of treatment any longer."

King agreed with Nixon. If the black community wouldn't stand up for the dignified and hardworking Rosa Parks, who would they support? That evening, more than fifty ministers and civic leaders gathered and threw their support behind a boycott of the buses to begin Monday. The ministers would spread the message Sunday at church services.

King returned from the meeting excited and energized. On Saturday, he and several workers produced thousands of leaflets to distribute throughout the black community.

"We are therefore asking every Negro to stay off the buses Monday in protest of the arrest and trial," one part read. "Don't ride the buses to work, to town, to school, or anywhere on Monday."

King remembered the biblical verse "He who accepts evil without protesting against it is really cooperating with evil."

But would Montgomery's blacks rally behind Parks? Would they have the discipline to stay off the buses? King fretted through a sleepless Sunday night. The first bus of the South Jackson Line would stop near his house at 6 A.M. Normally, it was packed.

At about 5:30 Monday morning, King rose, prepared a pot of coffee, and sat down at his kitchen table to wait. Coretta suddenly yelled to him from the front window. "Martin, Martin, come quickly!" she cried. King ran to the window and saw an empty bus drive away. Fifteen minutes later, another bus drove by—an empty shell.

King jumped in his car and drove the city's streets with growing excitement. The boycott appeared to be complete. Buses pulled in and out of stations, but no one boarded or got off. Above the roar of the engines and squeaky brakes of buses, groups of black youths happily sang out, "No riders today!"

King was moved by the scenes he saw—black students hitchhiking to school, laborers walking several miles to work, one black man riding a mule-drawn wagon.

The white city leaders were stunned. They raged among themselves, incapable of understanding that Montgomery blacks had mounted the boycott themselves. No, they reasoned, this was the work of outside agitators and the NAACP.

At 9 A.M., Rosa Parks went to court, where the judge fined her fourteen dollars for violating Montgomery's segregation ordinance. By appealing the court's decision, black leaders could now take the case on appeal before a federal court. And the federal court could decide whether segregation itself was constitutional.

A Boycott

The boycott leaders met that afternoon and created an organization to coordinate the protest—the Montgomery Improvement Association (MIA). They elected King president. King was taken aback by the offer. Just three weeks before, he had refused to run for presidency of the local NAACP.

When King hesitated, Nixon made it clear that

the job was his. "You ain't got much time to think," he said, "cause you in the chair from now on." King accepted.

When the meeting ended and King returned home, it was nearly 6 P.M. He feared telling his wife about the events of the meeting. She had already made sacrifices to come South, and now they were responsible for their two-week-old baby. But she took the news calmly. "You have my backing," she said.

With his wife and child. King was newly married and starting a family when he began fighting for civil rights.

Comforted by his wife's words, King looked at the clock—6:30. At 6:50, he would have to leave to attend the massive meeting planned for that night. As the president of the MIA, he would have to give a speech to justify the boycott. The responsibility came crushing down on him. Normally, he spent fifteen hours preparing for a sermon. Now, he had fifteen minutes to prepare for what could be the most important speech of his life.

King went to his study and hastily sketched an outline. He pondered how he would demand justice but not unleash the bitterness and rage of the black community—bitterness and rage that would lead to violence and thus destroy everything he was working for.

By the time he had dashed off a few notes, a friend, Elliot Finley, arrived to drive him to the rally. King sat in the driver's seat, pondering his speech when they abruptly halted in a traffic jam. The minutes lengthened. King suddenly realized that no cars were moving—the streets around the church were jammed. Dozens of cars had been parked and abandoned on sidewalks.

"You know something, Finley," said King as he swung the door open, "This could turn into something big."

Rallying the Crowd

Fifteen minutes later, King had made his way through the crowd and stood at the church's pulpit. Hundreds of expectant, eager faces looked up at him in hushed silence. People had packed into the pews and overflowed the balcony. Others crouched in the aisles, stood along the walls, and peeked in through the windows.

King paused and drew breath.

"We are here this evening," King began, "for serious business." Black Americans, he explained, were American citizens and entitled to their rights. Then he switched to Rosa Parks, speaking of her good character and the reason she had been jailed. The crowd murmured "yes" and "amen" in response.

Then King's voice rose. "And you know, my friends, there comes a time, when people get tired of being trampled over by the iron feet of oppression!" he cried. Individuals began to yell in response until it merged into an unbroken roar. The seated pounded their feet against the wooden floors until the church vibrated and rocked.

"The great glory of American democracy is the right to protest for right," King continued, at a lower volume. "There will be no crosses burned at any bus stops in Montgomery. There will be no white persons pulled out of their homes and taken out on some distant road and murdered."

"My friends, I want it to be known—that we're going to work with grim and bold determination—to gain justice in the buses in this city," he said, his voice rising in intensity. "And we are not wrong. We are not wrong in what we are doing. If we are wrong—the Supreme Court of this nation is wrong." People began shouting again in agreement, their voices unleashed by King's words. "If we are wrong—God Almighty is wrong!"

The shouts, the yells, the screams, rose, threatening to break over King. But King wasn't finished. "If we are wrong—Jesus of Nazareth was merely a utopian dreamer and never came down to earth! If we are wrong—justice is a lie."

The energy of the crowd exploded again, rocking off the walls, vibrating the floors, threatening to burst the church and pour into the city. "They were on fire for freedom," wrote a white reporter covering the speech, "There was a spirit there that no one could capture it again . . . it was so powerful."

Abernathy took the pulpit and read the MIA's demands: 1) bus drivers must treat black passengers with courtesy; 2) all seating must be first-come, first-serve, blacks from the rear, whites from the front; 3) the bus company must hire blacks to drive on predominantly black routes.

King asked the crowd if they supported the resolution. "All in favor, let it be known by standing on your feet," he said. As one, the crowd rose.

Changed Forever

Nothing would ever be the same after that night. As the exhausted King left the church, he did not know that he had made himself a national figure with one speech. He was just twenty-six years old.

Not only King was changed. Never had such a chorus of united protest been raised in Montgomery—the former cradle of the Confederacy. As the crowd flowed out of the church and walked back to their cars or homes, they felt a new spirit.

"The real victory was in the mass meeting," King later wrote in *Stride toward Freedom: The Montgomery Story*, "where thousands of black people stood revealed with a new sense of dignity and destiny."

King and other black leaders met with the white city leaders on December 8. At first, King believed that the white leaders would listen to reason. King spoke of the poor treatment given to black passengers and listed the MIA demands. But the city leaders refused to bend or change the city's segregation laws.

King left the meeting discouraged. He was disgusted with his earlier optimism and he realized that those in power would never compromise willingly. They must be forced.

The city leaders, however, believed the boycott was a joke.

"Comes the first rainy day," the mayor predicted with a sneer, "and the Negroes will be back on the buses."

The Boycott Continues

After one week, the buses were still empty. But black people still had to somehow get to work. Several black taxicab companies offered to take people for a cheap fare, but the city police commissioner threatened to arrest any cab driver who gave a ride for less than the standard forty-five cents. With taxis unable to help, King turned to carpooling. He announced his plan at a church meeting and asked members of the congregation to volunteer their cars. Almost 150 people responded. King was heartened but still staggered by the task before him. The blacks were boycotting between 30,000 and 40,000 fares per day. Each of the 150 cars would have to provide 130 rides a day just to make up 20,000 fares. King knew of a similar attempt to carpool during a boycott in Baton Rouge, Louisiana. It had collapsed after two weeks.

But a sense of injustice and commitment to the boycott had taken hold among Montgomery's blacks. One elderly black woman refused to ride with a car pool. She said she'd rather walk. "I'm not walking for myself," she said, "I'm walking for my children and my grandchildren."

King told another elderly black woman that everyone would understand if she returned to the buses. But she refused.

"My feet is tired, but my soul is rested," she said. Delighted, King would use the phrase as a rallying cry.

In the meantime, the bus company, based in Chicago, watched the number of fares tumble. While the city leaders claimed that the boycott was ineffective, the bus company managers cried out that they were nearing bankruptcy. Still, the city leaders refused to give in. Segregation was the law.

The MIA considered using its most explosive tactic—a lawsuit against bus segregation. Fred Gray, a black lawyer, began locating plaintiffs for the suit—most of them women who had been verbally abused by bus drivers. The only way such a suit could succeed is if it was filed in a federal court, away from the racist state courts.

Breaking the Boycott

In an effort to break the boycott, the Montgomery police began ticketing car-pool drivers. On January 26, 1956, King was driving a car pool when a motorcycle policeman stopped him.

"Get out, King," said the policeman. "You're under arrest for speeding thirty miles an hour in a twenty-five-mile zone."

King was packed into the back seat of a patrol car and rushed away. Panic seized him when the car drove away from the city. Often, the police dropped off black prisoners alone in the countryside, where a lynch mob awaited. King was overcome with relief when he finally glimpsed the sign for the jail.

King was pushed down a foul-smelling hallway and into a cell with several other prisoners. As the barred door slammed shut behind him, King felt disoriented. He had never been in jail before. News of King's arrest swept through Montgomery, and a huge crowd of blacks gathered outside the jail. Frightened by the demonstration, the jailer quickly released King on bail.

Rumors swirled through Montgomery, and several blacks swore violent revenge. No one could believe that King had been arrested. King held a mass meeting that night to explain what had happened to him and to urge that the community continue its nonviolent protest. Later that night, King received a phone call.

"Listen nigger," said the caller. "We've taken all we want from you. Before next week you'll be sorry you ever came to Montgomery."

Doubts, fears, and crushing expectations settled onto King. He sat at his kitchen table and prayed more devoutly than he ever had in his life. The pressure and strain were too much. He thought, "I've come to the point where I can't face it alone." At that moment, King later recalled, a feeling of peace flooded through him and radiated outward, melting his fears. An "inner voice" told him to do what he thought was right. King rose and returned to work.

Martin Luther King III watching his dad pull out a four-foot cross that was burned on their lawn. The cross was a warning from the Ku Klux Klan, a group of white supremacists.

Into the Federal Courts

On January 30, the MIA leaders voted to proceed with the federal lawsuit. That evening, King was preaching at Abernathy's church when he received horrifying news—his house had been bombed. King announced the news to the shocked congregation before driving home. He did not know if his children and wife were injured.

A line of nervous policemen stood outside his home in front of an angry mob. King passed through them, up his front steps and onto the porch, his feet crunching pieces of shattered glass. The living room was crowded with white city leaders, policemen, and black officials. King ignored them, went to a rear room and found Coretta and his children shaken but unharmed. Relieved that they were all right, King turned his attention back outside, where angry members of the crowd were yelling and pushing the policemen.

A panicked police officer came running into the living room, telling Reverand King that the growingly frightened and angry crowd refused to let anyone leave until King assured them that he was all right. King walked out onto the porch and held up his hand for silence.

Asking for calm. King begging the crowd to be peaceful after his home is bombed.

"Don't get panicky," he said. "Don't do anything panicky. Don't get your weapons . . . He who lives by the sword shall perish by the sword. . . . We must meet hate with love."

Later, policemen would say that they would have all been dead except for King's calming words.

February dawned cold. King was now receiving more than thirty hate letters a day. The phone rang constantly. Some of the calls were supporters to discuss strategy, but at least twenty of them angry, hate-filled voices cursing and threatening.

Floodlights lit King's home in a glare, and armed

sentries patrolled outside. In the first shock after the violence, King had agreed to let volunteer guards carry guns. But the decision disturbed him. Guns would only attract more guns, he reasoned, and he decided to ban them from his house. He would face the rising tide of hatred and violence with his philosophy of love.

At a crowded rally in Montgomery, whites, including all members of the city council, fiercely denounced the boycott. Racist pamphlets were handed out at the event. One read: "In every stage of the bus boycott we have been oppressed and degraded. . . . If we don't stop helping these African flesh-eaters, we will soon wake up and find Reverend King in the White House."

Anger, distrust, and resentment filled the city. "This is like war," said one black. "You can't trust anyone, black or white, unless you know him."

An Indictment

A white jury in Montgomery indicted King and all the leaders and drivers in the boycott. King was in Nashville when the news came. He flew to Atlanta for a connecting flight to Montgomery. But King's father had different ideas. As father and son drove home through Atlanta's streets, King Sr. ordered his son to stay in Atlanta. King Sr. had watched his son with a growing mixture of fear and pride. But the bombing and indictment were too much. King listened to his father with patience. Later, at home, he listened as old friends and mentors urged him to stay in Atlanta.

Finally, King interrupted. "I have to go back to Montgomery," he said. King Sr. burst into tears. The next morning, they packed into a car and drove to Montgomery. King was arrested at 9 A.M. with eighty-eight others. The city cited an old law that prohibited boycotting. King was tried on March 19 and convicted just three days later. The judge found King guilty and fined him five hundred dollars.

Outside the courthouse, King spoke to a cheering crowd of supporters. "The protest will go on!" he shouted. News of King's conviction spread around the globe. The boycott, now three months long, seized national and international attention. Reporters crowded into Montgomery and interviewed King, who described the struggle with eloquence and passion. King became a national figure—his face appeared on television and his speeches in newspapers.

In June, the protesters won a major victory when

A jubilant arrest. King and his wife grinning for cameras after he was arrested and fined for his part in the bus boycott.

a federal court in Alabama ruled that the Montgomery segregation laws were unconstitutional. The Montgomery lawyers appealed the case, sending it to the highest court in the land—the Supreme Court.

In the meantime, King began a speaking tour of the United States. He told "the Montgomery story" to enthusiastic audiences in packed halls and auditoriums. By October, King was exhausted, and the boycott dragged into its eleventh month. The car pool had developed into an intricate organization that was running smoothly.

Crushing the Car Pool

The city leaders tried to crush the boycott by turning their attention to the car pool. They sued the car pool in court, stating that it was a franchise—a business—operating without a city license. If the judge supported the city's case, then the car pool would be illegal, and all blacks would have to walk.

King was in despair. "I'm afraid our people will go back to the buses," he told his wife, "It's just too much to ask them to continue if we don't have the transportation for them."

On November 3, King sat at the defendant's table in court and listened gloomily as the city attorney's argued that the car pool was an illegal business. King was certain that the judge would rule in the city's favor.

"The clock said it was noon," he recalled, "but it was midnight in my soul." Suddenly, a reporter ran up to King with a note. "Here is the decision you have been waiting for," he said.

The note contained the latest news from Washington D.C., where the Supreme Court had ruled that segregation on buses was unconstitutional. The realization of what this meant surged through King and filled him with joy. It was over. The highest court in the land had declared the laws that separated black and white on buses illegal.

The news spread through the courtroom. One man couldn't restrain himself. "God Almighty has spoken from Washington D.C.!" he shouted. When order was restored, the judge made his ruling against the car pool, but it was pointless now.

Montgomery's black community went wild with celebration. The KKK, in a last bid to terrify blacks into submission, rode through the black section of Montgomery. Normally, KKK rides scared blacks into their homes behind locked doors. But this night, Montgomery's blacks turned on their lights and waved from their front porches.

"They acted as though they were watching a circus parade," said King, "No one fears the Klan or the White Citizen's Council."

On December 21, King and his close supporters climbed aboard the first integrated bus. Violence soon broke out. On December 28, white snipers began firing at the buses, hitting a pregnant black woman in her legs. On January 10, 1957, four churches and two pastors' homes were bombed. Again, King begged angry crowds to remain nonviolent.

The violence was the last gasp of bus segregation in

Montgomery. Blacks and whites returned to the buses, most of them riding peacefully. Many of the whites actually felt admiration for the black protesters.

"We've got to hand it to those Negroes," some later told *New York Times* reporter Abel Plenn. "They had principles and they stuck to them and they stuck together. They organized and planned well."

Founding The Southern Christian Leadership Conference

On January 11, King returned to Atlanta where he and other black ministers helped found an organization to bring together black churches in the cause of racial and social justice—the Southern Christian Leadership Conference (SCLC).

With the SCLC, King began an organized campaign to end racism in the South. The Montgomery bus boycott had done more than simply desegregate the city's buses; it had given the black community a new sense of pride and collective accomplishment. These feelings were stirring in black communities across the nation. No longer would blacks simply accept the place given them by white America. On buses, in schools, at lunch counters, blacks began a campaign to demand equal treatment.

WE SHALL
OVERCOME

THE BOYCOTT MADE King a national figure. In spring 1957, King and his wife
traveled to Africa. Most of Africa had
been ruled by white, European nations since
the 1800s. But in the 1950s, Africans rebelled
against European power and demanded the
right to rule themselves. In the African
nation of Ghana, King linked his struggle
against racism with the battle for equal rights
being waged around the world.

"Although we are separated by many
miles we are closer together in a mutual
struggle for freedom and human brother-

hood," he wrote to a group of African protesters. "We realize that injustice anywhere is a threat to justice everywhere."

When King returned to the United States, he held strategy conferences with other black leaders. Across the South, whites were resisting changes ordered by the Supreme Court. King and others implored President Dwight Eisenhower to speak to the nation and urge everyone to obey the law.

Meeting with the Vice President

On June 13, King and Abernathy met with Vice President Richard Nixon for more than two hours. King appealed to Nixon for Eisenhower to come to the South and make a speech supporting the Supreme Court decisions against segregation. Nixon offered to come in the president's place.

The president introduced the first civil rights legislation in Congress in eighty-two years. The legislation would strengthen the ability of blacks to vote. Southern congressmen bitterly resisted the bill. Strom Thurmond of South Carolina planned to delay the bill. He took the floor and began speaking, holding the floor for twenty-four continuous hours.

Majority leader Lyndon Johnson helped strip the

Meeting with Vice President Nixon. King urged Nixon and President Eisenhower to support the integration efforts.

bill of its power, and it passed in weakened form in August. King endorsed the Civil Rights Act of 1957 but learned an important lesson. To make change, blacks should rely more on themselves and less on white-controlled institutions.

King soon became president of the Southern Christian Leadership Conference. With the SCLC, King planned to use the nonviolent tactics he had learned in Montgomery to win justice for blacks across the nation. King also mobilized the SCLC to conduct voter registration drives to register blacks.

With the power of the vote, thought King, blacks could gain political power.

Another Crisis

Another race crisis threatened to engulf the nation. On September 9, nine black students attempted to enroll at all-white Central High School in Little Rock, Arkansas. Governor Orval Faubus responded by ordering soldiers from the National Guard to block their path. Frenzied whites yelled insults and stood by the soldiers to make sure that the black students did not make it through the school's doors.

For the first time since the Civil War, a military unit was resisting the federal government. In Washington, Eisenhower searched for a solution to the crisis. Eisenhower and Faubus struck a deal that the National Guard soldiers would switch from preventing the black students from entering the school to guarding them from the white mobs. But on September 23, the black students arrived to find that the National Guard had been ordered to leave. The students were surrounded by angry, screaming whites. Police desperately evacuated the students. The school remained segregated.

Eisenhower lost his patience. Seeing the crisis as a challenge to his authority, he ordered one thousand U.S. Army soldiers to Little Rock. Surrounded by the protective guns and bayonets, the nine students peacefully entered school the next morning.

King despaired over the violence of the confrontation, but he was heartened that the federal government had stepped in to help blacks at last.

King also urged that blacks seize power for themselves through the ballot box. In 1959, the SCLC began a massive voter registration drive. Almost 5 million blacks in the South were eligible to vote, but only 1.3 million were registered. King envisioned a solid voting block that could finally demand that its needs be met.

More Changes Shake the U.S.

As King struggled to implement the SCLC's programs, other changes shook the nation.

On February 1, 1960, four black students from Greensboro, North Carolina, walked into a Woolworth's and sat at the whites-only lunch counter. They launched a movement simply by ordering a cup of coffee. The white waitress refused, stating that they were sitting in the white section. That's OK, said the students, we'll sit and wait. They waited, even after the store closed and lights were shut off.

Waiting for equal treatment. This black college student in Birmingham, Alabama, participated in a sit-in and was eventually arrested.

Within weeks, similar demonstrations, called "sit-ins," erupted at segregated facilities in eleven southern cities. Students were now at the forefront of the civil rights movements. They adopted a song that would become the anthem of their movement, "We Shall Overcome."

We shall overcome,
We shall overcome,
We shall overcome some day,

Oh deep in my heart,
I do believe,
We shall overcome some day.

The 1960 Presidential Campaign

The civil rights movement became a big issue in the 1960 presidential campaign. Both Richard Nixon and his opponent, John F. Kennedy, battled to win the black vote. Kennedy promised to use the presidency to fight for civil rights. But in the summer of 1960, King refused to endorse either candidate. He remained skeptical that either would help blacks.

In October, with the election only two weeks away, King was arrested with a group of protesting students and thrown in jail. The students were soon released, but King was still on probation for driving without a Georgia driver's license. The judge ordered King to serve four months in jail.

Kennedy learned of the incident and called Coretta to express his sympathy. Kennedy's brother Robert, in the meantime, put pressure on the Atlanta judge. One day later, King was allowed to pay bail and leave. Kennedy's political advisers printed up two million pamphlets describing the call and distributed them in the black community.

On November 11, Kennedy was elected by a razor-thin margin. King said that blacks had provided Kennedy with the votes. Therefore, he should support the civil rights movement with federal power.

But Kennedy did not act. He did not want to alienate southern politicians, whose support he needed.

Impatient at Kennedy's reluctance to move, a group of students decided to force him. In 1960, the Supreme Court ruled segregation was illegal on interstate buses and in bus stations. But after a year, southern state governments simply ignored the order and kept the buses and stations strictly segregated. In May 1961, a group called the Freedom Riders bought bus tickets and began a bus ride into the South. At each terminal, they planned to have blacks enter the "white" area and whites to enter the "black" area.

Angry mobs awaited them. Outside Anniston, Alabama, the bus was blocked and set afire. The second bus raced on to Birmingham. When it arrived in the terminal, the Freedom Riders were savagely beaten with pipes and baseball bats by a screaming mob. The local police were nowhere to be seen.

A busload of Freedom Riders in Montgomery, Alabama. Many southern citizens were angered by the arrival of these activists.

As Kennedy tried to work out some sort of deal with the Alabama governor, another group of Freedom Riders set out. On May 20, the group arrived in Montgomery and departed from the bus into the quiet terminal. Suddenly, they were beaten mercilessly by another mob. King, watching the horrifying images on television, had seen enough.

Supporting the Freedom Riders

He went to Montgomery to stand with the students. The next evening, King addressed a crowd in Abernathy's church in support of the Freedom Riders. Outside, a white crowd gathered, seething with hate. In fury, they turned over a car and set it afire. Others threw rocks, shattering the stained glass windows. Inside, the congregation huddled in fear. King hurried to the basement and telephoned Robert Kennedy and said that a mob was going to burn down the church.

Kennedy told him not to worry, federal marshals were on their way. King went back upstairs and peeked outside. The marshals had arrived and were straining against the crowd. In a few hours, the marshals, reinforced by the National Guard, dispersed the mob, and the church members could finally go home.

After the Freedom Rides, the federal government renewed a crackdown on segregation on buses. Within two years, segregation on interstate travel was gone, a relic of the past.

King reflected on the enormous achievement of the students. Their courage, and the ugliness of the white mobs that tried to crush them, was captured

King and President Kennedy made many sacrifices in their fight for civil rights.

on television for the entire world. King realized that the mass media—newspapers, magazines, and most importantly, television—were critical for the success of the civil rights movement. When people could *see* the evil of racism, they would react. King learned this valuable lesson well and would use it in his next campaign.

THE BATTLE OF BIRMINGHAM

I N JANUARY 1963, one hundred years after Abraham Lincoln emancipated the slaves, the newly elected governor of the state of Alabama, George Wallace, told a cheering crowd at his inauguration, "Segregation now, Segregation tomorrow, Segregation forever!"

The more things changed in the South, the more they seemed to stay the same. After court decisions and the violence of the Freedom Rides, white southerners remained defiant and devoted to segregation. They blamed the civil rights movement on outsiders and a federal government that tyrannically trampled their rights.

The city of Birmingham, Alabama, proudly called itself a bastion of segregation. For several years, a local black leader had vainly tried to integrate the city's bus stations, schools, and lunch counters. The Klan enforced racism with savage violence, even bombing a black preacher's house on Christmas Eve after he protested the city's segregated buses. It was a city ruled by fear and hatred, and King described Birmingham as the "country's chief symbol of racial intolerance."

Therefore, thought King, it was the perfect target for protests. As Wallace loudly defended segregation, King and his advisers were secretly plotting to destroy it.

Project C

In January 1963, King and his closest advisers developed a plan, called Project C (the "C" stood for "confrontation"), to systematically end Birmingham segregation for good.

In the first phase of Project C, the movement would strike at the city's economy. Protesters would boycott, picket, and hold sit-ins in downtown stores

Part of Project C. Groups of African-Americans marched through Birmingham protesting segregation and unequal treatment.

to protest segregation and draw attention to their complaints. Hopefully, many of the store owners would react to the negative publicity.

In the second phase, the black community would participate in massive parades to city hall. In the third phase, black protesters, including King and other leaders, would voluntarily violate the law and be arrested. The masses of arrests would swamp the jails, and whites would be forced to confront the evil of segregation. The store owners would be forced to negotiate.

King and his aides urged their followers to reject violence. But they did not anticipate similar consideration from the police. The Birmingham police commissioner, Eugene "Bull" Connor, promised to arrest all protesters and vowed that "blood would run in the streets" before the city would desegregate.

The "Battle of Birmingham" began on April 3, when sixty-five blacks split into groups and asked for service at segregated lunch counters in five department stores. In four of the stores, the prepared waitresses simply turned off the lights and said that they were closed. In the fifth store, Connor's police hauled twenty-one blacks off to jail.

The demonstrations were roundly criticized. King issued the Birmingham Manifesto that listed the causes and hopes of the demonstrations. The press ignored it, instead poking fun at King's promise of massive demonstrations when in reality only twenty-one people had been arrested. Birmingham leaders blamed the protests on outsiders. In Washington, Robert Kennedy called them "ill-timed."

King and his aides expected much of the criticism from the press and city leaders, but they were not prepared for the many members of the black community who attacked King's tactics. They suggested that blacks give the new Birmingham mayor a chance. King was forced to spend days rallying black business leaders and preachers to his cause.

On April 6, protesters marched on city hall, the first wave of protests that would last thirty-four consecutive days. Forty-five people were arrested. But the protests were not attracting media attention, and the pool of blacks willing to be arrested and go to jail was beginning to dry up. Worse, the funds used to bail the protesters out of jail were critically low.

King preached every night in packed churches, asking for volunteers. When they came forward, they took part in special sessions. They were trained to absorb cursing and beatings without striking back. Only nonviolence, preached King, could win over the conscience of the nation.

On April 11, Connor won a court order that stated that further demonstrations were illegal. King now prepared for the pivotal moment in the two weeks of protest—his own arrest. For the first time, King prepared to defy a court order. He stated that the law itself was unjust and must be disobeyed. But devastating news arrived—the organization had run out of money for bail. Without bail money, King and his followers could languish for weeks, maybe months, in jail.

King's advisers argued heatedly over whether King should still go to jail. The organization needed money, said one adviser, and King should go on a speaking tour to raise it. "If you go to jail," he added, "the battle of Birmingham is lost."

Agonizing over a decision, King entered an adjoining room and shut the door to be alone. No protest can succeed without money, King realized. But he had also promised to go to jail. He contemplated the people in the movement, the ones who had sung as they walked into the city's prison cells. Within minutes, King made his decision. He dressed in faded blue overalls and a blue denim shirt and emerged from the room.

"I'm going to jail," he told his silent advisers. "I don't know what will happen. I don't know where the money will come from. But I have to make a faith act."

That evening, with Abernathy and fifty others, King marched down to city hall. There, surrounded by police and barricades, King came face to face with Connor. King and Abernathy knelt in prayer. The police swarmed over the protesters and carried

Marching toward city hall. King and Ralph Abernathy (at head of line) led a group of protesters in Birmingham but were stopped by police.

them by the seat of their pants to trucks waiting to take them to prison. For the thirteenth time, King was arrested.

Frustrating Jail Time

King was taken to a narrow, murky jail cell without a mattress, pillow, or blanket. His jailers refused his requests to talk to his lawyers or make phone calls. Alone in the quiet darkness, King fretted about the movement and desperately awaited news.

"Those were the longest, most frustrating hours I have ever lived," King wrote later in a book about the protest, *Why We Can't Wait*. "I was in a nightmare of despair."

Friday night passed and on Saturday King met briefly with a lawyer to make sure he was all right. Saturday dragged into Sunday. By now, King was exhausted, lonely, and depressed. But on Monday morning, King was delighted to see Clarence Jones at his cell door. Jones, a lawyer from New York, had important news.

"Harry [Belafonte] has been able to raise fifty thousand dollars for bail bonds," he said. "It is available immediately. And he said that whatever else you need, he will raise it."

King's gamble had worked. As he had hoped, the organization had received the money it needed to continue the protests. "I cannot express what I felt," King wrote in *Why We Can't Wait*, "but I knew at that moment that God's presence had never left me, that He had been with me there in solitary."

Jones's words, King wrote, had lifted "a thousand pounds from my heart."

King was allowed to call his wife, who told him that President Kennedy had called her to express

King with Harry Belafonte. The entertainer helped King and his movement by providing money for bail bonds.

his personal concern. King told her to tell the press.

Back in his cell, King read a letter printed in a newspaper written by six white clergymen. They criticized the movement and King, and urged blacks to take their protests off the streets and into the courtroom. Incensed by criticism from other ministers, King began to write a response on paper smuggled into the jail.

The ministers accused King of being an outsider. King responded that the fight for justice goes on everywhere.

The ministers urged blacks to have more patience. Change was coming, they said. King fired back that blacks have been waiting for decades and could wait no longer for rights they deserved long ago.

The ministers pointed out that King had broken laws. King responded that there exist two kinds of laws: just and unjust. Segregation laws were unjust, and each citizen had the duty to break unjust laws.

The ministers criticized the movement's tactics of sit-ins and massive arrests, calling them too extreme. King noted that his tactics were nonviolent. He pointed out that many blacks wished to end segregation by violently tearing down the entire system. Whites, King warned, should support the nonviolent movement to prevent the nightmare of a race war.

King arranged for twenty pages to be smuggled out of the jail. His advisers typed them up in excitement, realizing that the letter was becoming a classic document for the civil rights movement. They called it "Letter from the Birmingham Jail."

Release from Jail

After eight days, King and Abernathy left prison. Both were exhausted and appeared haggard, their faces shadowed by beards. King was horrified to learn that the demonstrations had dwindled into minor protests. Pressure was still on the Birmingham business owners, but King knew that more was needed to begin negotiations. Bigger marches were needed. But after another week, the protests had all but collapsed.

For a month, King had thrown himself into the protests, even offering to be jailed. Nothing had worked. King and the SCLC, with a $1 million budget and more than one hundred workers, appeared doomed to a devastating defeat.

Desperate, SCLC organizers canvased local high schools, attracting hundreds of students to march. Younger children in the elementary schools saw their older brothers and sisters volunteer and begged to be included.

King pondered including the children. He knew he would draw fierce criticism for placing children in what could become a dangerous situation. But Birmingham needed a jolt—some action to revive the protests and revive the conscience of the nation. King gave the order.

A Thousand Child March

On May 2, more than one thousand children, some as young as six, began marching from the Sixteenth Street Baptist Church toward downtown Birmingham. They went in columns, singing and clapping with joy. The police arrested them at a frantic pace, packed them into school buses, and hauled them to jail. By the end of the day, the exhausted police had arrested more than nine hundred people. Groups of seventy-five children had been crammed into cells that usually held eight. Now there was no more space. The children of Birmingham had filled the jails.

News spread like wildfire through the city. At the church meeting that evening, King told one thousand listeners, "I have been moved today. I have never seen anything like it. If they think this is the end of this, they are sadly mistaken."

The next morning, more than 2,500 school children gathered at the Sixteenth Street Baptist Church.

In the streets around the church, police and fireman stood at their roadblocks alongside journalists and photographers. The police had orders to keep the marchers contained near the church. The city's K-9 unit was on call, their vicious dogs straining at their leashes. The firemen mounted powerful hoses on tripods. With these hoses, they could knock apart bricks or strip bark from a tree at 100 feet.

A column of schoolchildren poured out of the church, singing and clapping as they turned toward the barricades. Furious, Bull Connor ordered the group to turn back. Instead the group began shouting, "We want freedom!"

Connor turned to the fire fighters and yelled, "Let 'em have it!"

The jets of water crashed into the column, slamming into adults and children alike, sweeping them back down the street. The high-pressure water tore clothing from bodies, pinned demonstrators up against walls, and knocked them to the ground.

A powerful black businessman watched the scene in an office high above the park.

"They've turned the fire hoses on a little black girl," he said in astonishment. "And they're rolling that girl right down the middle of the street."

The violence in Birmingham escalated as police used harsher tactics with the demonstrators.

The columns disintegrated into confusion as protesters fled the onslaught, their songs of freedom turning to howls of pain and rage. In fury, nearby blacks began throwing bottles and rocks at the firemen. Connor unleashed the dogs. Fangs snapping, German shepherds lunged into the crowd, mauling three children. Bloodied and soaked, the protesters streamed back to the church.

By 3 P.M., it was over. Dozens of protesters had been wounded and 250 arrested. King ordered the marches to cease. If what happened in Birmingham that day did not stir the conscience of the nation, then nothing would.

Aftermath of the March

The next morning, Americans picked up their newspapers and saw searing images printed across the front page—the protesters, children blasted with water, a dog biting into a man's abdomen. Readers recoiled in horror. President Kennedy said that the pictures made him "sick." Across Africa, Europe, and the United States, a storm of criticism poured down on Bull Connor and the leaders of Birmingham.

The civil rights movement was never the same again. Shamed and stirred by the sacrifice of their children, black adults swelled the ranks of the protests by the thousands. The marches continued and the chants only grew louder, "We want freedom!" Bull Connor continued to unleash his dogs and hoses on the protesters, and the jails filled, until more than three thousand were locked up.

In the meantime, the business leaders of Birmingham were finally willing to negotiate. The protests had severely damaged the city's reputation in the United States and abroad. Unless something was done, the city's economy would be severely crippled.

On May 10, King and the business community reached an agreement. Every lunch counter, restroom, drinking fountain, and fitting room would be desegregated within ninety days. Blacks would be hired as clerks, salespeople, and managers within sixty days.

"The city of Birmingham has reached an accord with its conscience," said King at a packed news conference. "Birmingham may well offer . . . an example of progressive racial relations; and for all mankind, a dawn of a new day."

Violence Threatens the Agreement

But a flare of violence threatened the historic agreement. Angry whites bombed the house where King was staying, injuring no one but causing a riot as angry blacks sought vengeance. King took to the streets, trying to calm the boiling rage that threatened to spill into the streets and ignite a race war.

President Kennedy announced that he would not let extremists ruin the pact. He ordered three thousand federal troops into a position near Birmingham. They were never needed. The bombings stopped and Birmingham slowly began a new era.

The events of Birmingham made King a hero throughout the country and the world. In Chicago, he rode through the city in an open limousine and was welcomed by the mayor himself as "the hero of Birmingham." In Hollywood, King was invited to a Beverly Hills party hosted by Charlton Heston, one of the most popular actors of his time. Heston and other actors donated thousands of dollars to the SCLC.

Protests against segregation erupted across the nation in the next few weeks. When someone finally counted them all, there had been 758 racial demonstrations and 14,733 arrests in 186 cities.

PEACE PRIZE

Oₙ June 11, in response to Birmingham and the growing unrest, President Kennedy gave a televised speech that was watched throughout the nation.

"We are confronted primarily with a moral issue," declared Kennedy. "It is as old as the Scriptures and is as clear as the American Constitution. The heart of the question is whether all Americans are to be afforded equal rights and equal opportunities, whether we are going to treat our fellow Americans as we want to be treated."

He asked his audience whether everyone could enjoy rights, except for blacks.

"Now the time has come for this nation to fulfill its promise. The events in Birmingham and elsewhere have so increased the cries for equality that no city or state or legislative body can prudently choose to ignore them."

King was delighted with the speech. At last, the president had forcefully thrown the weight of his office behind the civil rights struggle.

Kennedy announced that he would introduce civil rights legislation in Congress. But King knew that the determined congressmen from the South would sink the bill. To pressure them, King and other civil rights leaders began to plan a march, a gathering in Washington D.C. itself to demonstrate to Congress the need for the legislation.

Kennedy was unenthusiastic, and white alarmists predicted a riot that would destroy the city.

March on Washington

On August 28, more than 250,000 people gathered on the Washington Mall. One by one, performers and civil rights leaders sang songs and gave speeches on a stage in front of the Lincoln Memorial.

The March on Washington. King waved to the huge crowd that had gathered at the Washington Mall in August 1963.

King spoke last. The previous night, he had wrestled with the wording of his speech, pressured by the need to say the right things at a truly historic moment. Because of the large number of speakers, each could speak for only eight minutes. King rehearsed the speech in his mind as he sat on the platform until finally he was called to the microphones to speak.

King spoke first of the evils of segregation, racism, and poverty. He then turned to nonviolence as a solution to the evils that beset American society. As he spoke, dozens of cameras carried King's words and image into millions of homes.

Then, in a burst of inspiration, King swerved off his planned text and began preaching from the heart, saying what he had wanted to say all along:

> *I have a dream, that one day this nation will rise up and live out the true meaning of its creed: "We hold these truths to be self evident—that all men are created equal." I have a dream that one day on the red hills of Georgia sons of former slaves and the sons of former slaveowners will be able to sit down together at the table of brotherhood. I have a dream that one day even the state of Mississippi, a state sweltering with the heat of injustice, sweltering with the heat of oppression, will be transformed into an oasis of freedom and justice. I have a dream that my four little children will one day live in a nation where they will not be judged by the color of their skin but by the content of their character.*

King continued on, the gospel singer Mahalia Jackson chanting, "My Lord! My Lord!" behind him. Finally, King approached the end.

"And when this happens," he said, "we will be able to speed up that day when all God's children, black men and white men, Jews and Gentiles,

"I Have a Dream." Many were inspired by the words of King's most famous speech.

Protestants and Catholics, will be able to join hands and sing in the words of the old Negro spiritual, 'Free at last! Free at last! Thank God Almighty, we are free at last!"

King stepped aside, drained from the effort and emotionally numbed. Abernathy hugged him, telling him that the Holy Spirit had inspired him.

In November, King was shocked to hear that President Kennedy had been assassinated in Dallas, Texas. As the nation grieved, King blamed a "climate of hate" for the death.

The new president, Lyndon B. Johnson, took up the cause to have civil rights legislation passed. He told Congress that passing the legislation would honor Kennedy's memory.

The Civil Rights Act

After months of negotiations and tense compromises, the Civil Rights Act was passed in July. The act outlawed discrimination based on race at pools, parks, hotels, theaters, or any other place of business. Never again could anyone put up a sign that said WHITES ONLY.

King was present when President Lyndon B. Johnson signed the Civil Rights Act into law on July 2, 1964.

King's popularity soared, and wherever he stayed he was mobbed by crowds, often to the point where he simply stayed in his hotel room.

King also drew the attention of the Federal Bureau of Investigation (FBI), who were convinced he was a communist. They tapped his phone line and placed microphones in his motel rooms.

Then came the highest honor. In October 1964, King was awarded the Nobel Peace Prize for his non-violent protests. The civil rights movements and the cause of black Americans was now recognized and honored on the international stage.

King's parents, wife, and sister flew to Norway to attend the Nobel Peace Prize ceremony.

SELMA

KING DID NOT TAKE the triumph as an excuse to relax. For several years, King, the SCLC, and other civil rights organizations had mounted a campaign to get blacks to vote. The results, however, had been disappointing.

Blacks had been given the right to vote after the Civil War. But southern legislatures passed laws that made registering almost impossible for blacks. To register, blacks had to recite large sections of the constitution by memory and answer dozens of questions. In other parts of the South, registering meant putting your life at risk or losing your job.

In Selma, Alabama, only 156 blacks were registered out of 15,000 of voting age. Blacks lived in a section of the city where the streets were unpaved clay and dirt. Poverty was rampant. Student groups organized rallies to register voters, but they met with harassment from the police and local whites.

King decided that Selma was the ideal spot to launch his new campaign to empower blacks across the South through voting. As he had in Birmingham, King planned to show the climate of hatred and racism in Selma to the world. The American people and the government would be forced to act.

Project Alabama

On January 2, 1965, King started Project Alabama, when he addressed a packed church in Selma. "Our cry to the state of Alabama is a simple one: Give us the ballot!" shouted King. "We're not on our knees begging for the ballot. We are demanding the ballot!"

The marches began the next day and continued through the week. Groups of blacks would gather at Brown Chapel and walk down to the courthouse to demand the right to vote. The courthouse was protected by Sheriff Jim Clark, a man who vowed to

King and a group of demonstrators marching from Selma to Montgomery in 1965. Police halted the march.

protect the "southern way of life" and not let blacks "take over the whole state of Alabama."

The police met the first demonstrators with restraint. But when the marches continued, Clark began to lose patience. On February 1, he arrested King and several hundred protesters, including 500 school children.

In the Selma jail, King wrote a letter that was published in the *New York Times*. "Why are we in jail?" he asked. "There are more Negroes in jail with me than there are on the voting rolls."

President Johnson gave a press conference on television, stating that no one should be denied the right to vote. After leaving jail, King met briefly with Johnson and urged him to support a bill that guaranteed voting rights. Back in Selma, one of King's advisers, James Bevel, suggested that they march 50 miles (80 kilometers) from Selma to Montgomery to demand voting rights. King liked the idea and plans were made to start the march on Sunday. But King begged off, stating that he had neglected his own pulpit in Montgomery. He assumed the marchers would be arrested and King planned to join them in jail.

On March 7, more than six hundred marchers gathered at the Brown Chapel in Selma. Toting bedrolls and tents, they walked out of the church and crossed a bridge onto Highway 80, the route to Montgomery. There, they saw a chilling sight. Three lines of helmeted state troopers, armed with clubs and tear gas, blocked the road. Governor Wallace had learned of the march, and the idea of hundreds of protesting blacks flooding into the state capital was too much. He ordered state troopers to block the march.

The black marchers approached the wall of police.

"You are ordered to disperse," shouted an officer. "Go home or go to your church. This march will not continue. You have two minutes."

After one minute, the police moved forward in a wave and slammed into the crowd, kicking, punching, and swinging their clubs with savage force. The first ranks of marchers collapsed, men and women alike beaten to the ground. Tear gas was fired, and the marchers still on their feet streamed back into the streets of Selma as crowds of white onlookers whooped and hollered with delight.

Police mounted on horseback rode into the mass, lashing out with whips and clubs. "Please, no!" screamed one marcher. "God, we're being killed."

Regular television programming was suddenly interrupted, and the images of policemen beating the marchers filled homes across America. The images shook the country to its core. Demonstrations against the brutality erupted in cities. In Detroit, ten thousand marched in support of voting rights and the Selma black community. Another two thousand gathered in Toronto, Ontario. Fifty congressmen took the floor of the House and Senate to denounce the attack. The incident was remembered as Bloody Sunday.

Demonstrators in Selma were attacked by mounted police officers in March 1965. Images such as these were broadcast on television and shocked the nation.

King sent out hundreds of telegrams, urging the religious leaders of the United States to come and march against such obvious evil. King was stunned by the response. More than four hundred clerics, priests, nuns, rabbis, and students gathered in Selma.

On Tuesday, King led 1,500 marchers out to the highway and faced the wall of police. But this time, King turned the group around, not wishing to provoke more violence. King's action, however, angered many of his supporters, who felt that he had backed down.

That night, a young white minister was beaten to

death. A huge outcry of grief and rage rose up from the nation again. Newspaper editorials demanded legislation to guarantee voting rights.

On March 15, President Johnson appeared on television. He stated, "What happened in Selma is part of a far larger movement . . . the effort of American Negroes to secure for themselves the full blessings of American life. Their cause is our cause too. Because it is not just Negroes, but really it is all of us, who must overcome the crippling legacy of bigotry and injustice."

At this moment, Johnson paused and then said deliberately, "And, we shall overcome!"

King watched the speech silently. When a friend looked over to see his reaction, she noticed tears running down his cheeks.

On March 21, 300 marchers began the 50-mile (80-km) trek to Montgomery as a civil rights army to lay siege to a capital where the Confederate flag flew overhead. With the world watching, they entered the state capital in triumph five days later. They arrived 25,000 strong, the largest civil rights demonstration in southern history.

"We are on the move now," King told the crowd, "Yes, we are on the move and no wave of racism can stop us."

A success. On March 21, 1965, King and a group of marchers trekked to Montgomery and held a huge civil rights demonstration.

The Voting Rights Act

In August 1965, King joined President Johnson in the rotunda of the U.S. Capitol, where Johnson signed the Voting Rights Act of 1965 into law. The act empowered the federal government to protect the rights of blacks to vote. King was jubilant.

Selma marked an end and a beginning. For King, it was his finest hour. Nine years earlier, few would have thought this possible. As a legal institution, segregation had been virtually abolished. Blacks could now vote in heavy numbers and control their own destiny.

But unknown to King in 1965, America was entering a period of social unrest that would break apart the civil rights movement and challenge King's dream of nonviolent change.

CRUSADE FOR THE POOR

FLUSH WITH HIS VICTORIES in the South, King now looked to the North. Segregation did not exist in the North as it had in the South, but blacks were kept out of many jobs and neighborhoods. The only thing missing was a sign that stated the obvious—WHITES ONLY.

King decided to go to Chicago. Like many American cities, Chicago had a large black population. They lived in cramped, deteriorating slums where they were forced to pay unreasonably high rents. Unemployment was severe, the schools inferior.

Summer Rioting

In the summers, the cities became pressure cookers with no pools or clean parks to release tension. In August 1965, black rage exploded in deadly riots in the Watts section of Los Angeles. Thirty-four people were killed, 3,500 injured and $46 million worth of property destroyed.

King saw the riots as inevitable, considering the crushing racism throughout American society. He resolved to launch a new campaign to rescue the

Reading the headlines. King felt that the race riots were inevitable given the conditions under which many African-Americans lived.

blacks from their urban prisons and prevent more riots.

In January 1966, King led an army of SCLC staffers into Chicago. His goal was simple: "Our primary objective will be to bring about the unconditional surrender of forces dedicated to the creation and maintenance of slums."

King moved his family into a slum house while he managed his campaign. He came face to face with the privations of slum life. The refrigerator broke and the heaters barely worked, even as the temperature outside plunged near zero. King took tours of the Chicago black ghetto, carefully observing the grim lives crushed by poverty.

But the campaign bogged down. King was facing a far different situation than in the South. In Chicago, Mayor Richard J. Daley shrewdly maneuvered around King. Other groups grumbled that King should concentrate on improving the schools. The press and other leaders wondered what King, a civil rights leader, was doing preaching about poverty anyway.

But to King, racism and poverty were intermixed—two halves of the same coin. How could blacks improve their lives if they couldn't get decent jobs, attend good schools, and live in secure, decent housing?

As King battled Richard J. Daley and Chicago, a civil rights worker on a solitary march for voting rights was shot in Mississippi. King and other civil rights activists pledged to continue the march.

As King made plans with the other civil rights activists, he noticed a new, angrier tone. While singing "We Shall Overcome," a group of young black civil rights activist sang "We Shall Overrun" instead.

King was puzzled. "My hearing was not attuned to the sound of such bitterness," he later wrote. The young activists were tired—tired of being shot at, tired of promises unfulfilled. One activist said that they should break the legs off the Statue of Liberty and throw her into the Mississippi River.

King pleaded with them, urging them to use non-violence. But as the march progressed, clusters of whites appeared, jeering and waving Confederate flags. Some of the blacks responded by singing, "Jingle Bells, shotgun shells, Freedom all the way, Oh what fun, it is to blast, A trooper man away."

One young activist, Stokey Carmichael, spoke of a new kind of rage to a crowd of supporters. "The only way we're going to stop them white men from whuppin' us is to take over," he said, "We been saying freedom for six years, and we ain't got nothin.' What we gonna start saying now is Black Power!"

The crowd chanted "Black Power" over and over again. King and his supporters were horrified. The civil rights movement, unified by King under the doctrine of nonviolence, was breaking apart. King understood their anger and impatience. But he could not excuse the use of violence.

Stokely Carmichael addressing a group of Black Power supporters. King was displeased with the violent attitude some groups encouraged.

Still, what could he expect? In America, violence seemed to be the solution. In 1965, the nation was slowly pulled into a war, when President Johnson began sending large numbers of American soldiers to a small country in Southeast Asia called South Vietnam. The country of Vietnam was torn by war between the communists in North Vietnam and the government supported by the United States in the South Vietnam.

Johnson was determined to defeat the communists. The American army in Vietnam swelled to more than 300,000 soldiers. At first, few Americans seemed concerned. King, however, watched the buildup with alarm. How could he preach nonviolence when his own country was waging war?

King felt the need to condemn America's role in Vietnam, but his advisers begged him to stay quiet and concentrate on civil rights. If he criticized the war, then he would alienate himself from Johnson and most of the American people.

Speaking out against the War

But King couldn't stay silent. In interviews, speeches, and conversations, King spoke out, stating the United States had no place killing Vietnamese.

The reaction was hostile. Newspaper columnists told King to avoid foreign policy and stick to civil rights. Johnson was furious.

King's outspoken stand on Vietnam cost him support as he continued to lead protests in Chicago. He was also losing support among young blacks, who were tired of his endless pleas for nonviolence.

Against the war. King joined others in protesting the American involvement in the Vietman War.

On Sunday, July 10, King spoke to 30,000 people in Chicago's Soldier Field, urging them to boycott banks and businesses that discriminated against blacks. He also called for massive nonviolent protests to fill the jails and force change. After the speech, he marched to city hall, where he taped a list of demands to the door. The action copied Martin Luther, who in 1517 nailed a list of demands to the door of a Catholic church, thus beginning the Protestant Reformation.

The Chicago Riots

On July 13, Chicago was rocked by riots. Groups of policeman marched up and down streets, while blacks pelted them with rocks and flaming bottles filled with gasoline. King drove through the city, pleading with groups to stop rioting. But it did little good. By the next day, 2 people were dead, 56 injured, and 282 arrested. The governor ordered 4,000 soldiers into the city to restore order.

Sadly, King's prediction had come true. He had seen the rage that had exploded into riots. He had pleaded with the city government to do something. But instead, the mayor blamed King and "outside" interference for the violence.

Members of the National Guard were called in to take control during Chicago's 1966 riots.

King refused to give up his campaign. On August 5, he led a march of six hundred blacks and whites into Chicago's white neighborhoods, where blacks were uninvited and unwanted.

Crowds gathered along the parade route to shriek at the marchers, wave Confederate flags, and chant "White Power!" The crowd began showering the marchers with rocks. One struck King above his right ear, sending him tumbling to the ground. But he quickly gained his feet and rejoined the march.

"I've never seen anything like it," King said later. "I can say that I have never seen—even in Mississippi and Alabama—mobs as hostile and hate-filled as I've seen in Chicago."

King continued the marches into white neighborhoods to expose the festering racism.

Finally, Mayor Daley and Chicago's business interests gave in. Banks agreed to loan money to all qualified people, regardless of color. The city promised to strictly enforce codes that allowed blacks and whites equally into housing.

Still, King and his aides were frustrated. The protests in Chicago had been exhausting. In the sleepy cities of the South, the marches won huge attention to King's causes. But King's protests in Chicago were almost lost against the busy backdrop of daily life in the city. King was also drained and discouraged by the complex problems of poverty. He saw poverty as the underlying root cause of social ills as America turned its back on its poor. King was determined to make the country finally pay attention.

FREE AT LAST

9

A S KING PLOTTED his next move, the nation seemed to come apart around him. One by one, American cities exploded in riots and chaos—in Atlanta, in Milwaukee, in Cleveland and in thirty-nine other cities. The war in Vietnam went on. American soldiers were locked in combat with North Vietnamese and guerrilla forces, and American bombers dumped tons of explosives on North Vietnamese cities. In January, the Communists waged a stunning counterattack that left America shaken in its belief that it could win the war.

As the country exploded into protests and riots, King planned his greatest, most ambitious project. In an attempt to force the United States to care for its poor, King dreamed of a march on Washington larger than the civil rights march in 1963. People of all colors and races would join him in nonviolent protests to disrupt the government itself.

The Weight of the Fight

King's plan was met with a tidal wave of criticism and fury. Johnson promised to mobilize 25,000 troops if King planned to enter *his* city. Radical blacks said he was doing too little. Moderate blacks feared he was doing too much. Assassination threats against King grew, until the FBI had recorded fifty.

Depression weighed on King as he labored through the spring of 1968 to bring his plan together. In Memphis, Tennessee, garbage workers were trying to organize a union in the face of hostile city authorities. In March, King met with the garbage workers and told them to strike.

On March 28, King returned to lead a march through the city. But blacks intent on making violence rioted during the march. King was mortified. He had never led a march that broke into social disorder. King returned to the city in April, determined to prove that nonviolent tactics still had meaning.

But King was shaken and the weight of his project bore down on him. On the night of April 3, he preached to a Memphis congregation about the growing threats to his life. His plane had been delayed in Atlanta as officers searched for bombs. Other threats warned him that he would meet his death in Memphis.

"But it really doesn't matter with me now," he said, "because I have been to the mountaintop. . . . And I've looked over, and I've seen the promised land. I may not get there with you. But I want you to know tonight that we, as a people, will get the to the promised land. So I'm happy tonight. I'm not worried about anything. I'm not fearing any man. Mine eyes have seen the glory of the coming of the Lord!"

The Final Day

The next morning—April 4—King rose from his sleep in his hotel room. He spent the day in planning sessions for the coming protests. Around 5:30 P.M. King and his advisers prepared to go to dinner. While Abernathy put on some aftershave lotion,

King walked out onto the hotel balcony and joked with some of his advisers in the parking lot below.

Suddenly, a single shot echoed. A bullet slammed into King's face and crumpled him to the balcony floor.

"Oh my god!" cried Abernathy. "Martin's been shot!"

An ambulance rushed King to a nearby hospital, where doctors cut open his chest and massaged his heart in a desperate bid to save his life. But the damage was too severe. At 7:05 P.M., doctors pronounced King dead.

Abernathy stood in the waiting room, too stunned to move. Later, authorities would capture a white man who was seen fleeing the scene of the crime named James Earl Ray.

But no one cared about that now. News of King's assassination spread through the nation and around the world. Riots exploded in 110 cities, killing thirty-nine people and requiring 75,000 federal troops and National Guardsmen to restore order.

The *New York Times* called King's murder a "national disaster." President Johnson declared April 7 a day of national mourning, and the flag fluttered at half-mast across the country.

Outpourings of grief came in from abroad. Pope Paul VI sent a cablegram expressing his "profound sadness." The British House of Commons introduced resolutions expressing their grief. In West Germany, the parliament observed a moment of silence for the slain civil rights leader.

On April 8, thousands of people walked by King's casket in Atlanta. Of all the tears shed that day, perhaps the most poignant were those from his father. "M.L.!" he cried at the casket. "Answer me, M.L. He never hated anybody, he never hated anybody."

The next day, the day of the funeral, 800 people packed into Ebenezer Baptist Church while more than 60,000 filled the streets outside. Between the eulogies and speeches in King's honor, a tape of King was played.

"If any of you are around when I have to meet my day," he said, "I don't want a long funeral . . . I'd like someone to mention that day that Martin Luther King Jr. tried to give his life serving others. I'd like for somebody to say that Martin Luther King Jr. tried to love somebody.

"I want you to be able to say that day that I did try to feed the hungry. I want you to be able to say that I did try in my life to clothe the naked. I want

Coretta Scott King at her husband's casket. Thousands of people attended King's funeral on April 9, 1968.

you to say on that day I did try in my life to visit those who were in prison. And I want you to say that I tried to love and serve humanity."

The coffin was loaded onto a farm wagon drawn by two mules that King had intended to use in his campaign for the nation's poor. Now, it carried him through the streets of Atlanta, followed by tens of thousands of mourners, supporters, and world leaders, winding its way until it reached the cemetery where King was laid to rest.

On the tombstone were inscribed King's name, the years of his birth and death, and a phrase from one his favorite Negro spirituals:

"Free at last, Free at last,

Thank God Almighty I'm free at last"

At the grave of Martin Luther King Jr. In many respects, he was finally "free at last."

THE LEGACY OF DR. KING

BEFORE MARTIN LUTHER KING JR., the United States was divided into two societies—one white, one black. They were separated by hatred, fear, misunderstanding, and the horrifying legacy of slavery and racism.

In the 1950s and 1960s, King worked to bridge the divide between the two societies and win rights for black Americans. Great changes in history usually result from violent force. But despite the poisoned, angry social atmosphere he often confronted, King never resorted to violence or succumbed to bitterness.

King spent most of his life working for civil rights. His efforts have made him one of the most respected people in U.S. history.

When King died from an assassin's bullet in 1968, many of the barriers that had stood against black Americans for decades had been removed. His non-violent tactics had caused a social revolution without bloody upheaval. That revolution to achieve equal rights for all Americans continues to this day.

King's legacy has only grown. In a recent poll, Americans voted King as the greatest role model of their times. King has joined the national heroes George Washington and Abraham Lincoln as one of three Americans to be honored with a national holiday.

TIMELINE

1929	Martin Luther King Jr. born on January 15 in Atlanta
1944	Enters Morehouse College at the age fifteen
1948	Is ordained as a minister on February 25; enrolls at Crozer Theological Seminary
1951	Graduates from Crozer; begins graduate work at Boston University
1952	Meets Coretta Scott, whom he later marries
1954	Accepts the position of pastor at Dexter Avenue Baptist Church in April
1955	Receives his doctorate degree; participates in and encourages the boycott of Montgomery buses; becomes president of the Montgomery Improvement Association
1956	Is arrested at various times for his part in the bus boycott; his home is bombed on January 30; on November 3, the Supreme Court rules that segregated buses are unconstitutional; rides the first integrated bus in Montgomery on December 21

1957	On January 11, helps found the Southern Christian Leadership Conference (SCLC) and later becomes its president; travels to Africa with his wife; on June 13, meets with Vice President Richard Nixon about the progress of integration
1959	The SCLC begins a voter registration drive
1960	In October, is arrested with a group of protestors; receives support from John F. Kennedy and is released from jail; backs Kennedy for president
1961	Speaks in support of the Freedom Riders
1963	In January, begins Project C; on April 11, is arrested again; receives bail money from Harry Belafonte; writes "Letter from the Birmingham Jail"; on August 28, delivers his "A Have a Dream" speech
1964	The Civil Rights Act is passed in July; receives the Nobel Peace Prize
1965	In January, begins Project Alabama; on March 21, leads a group protesters on a march from Selma to Montgomery; in August, the Voting Rights Act is signed into law
1966	Moves with his family to a slum in Chicago; speaks out against the U.S. role in the Vietnam War; race riots break out throughout the country
1968	Begins to plan another march on Washington; receives death threats; on April 4, is shot and killed in Memphis

HOW TO BECOME A MINISTER

The Job

Protestant ministers provide for the spiritual, educational, and social needs of Protestant congregations and other people of the community. They lead services, perform religious rites, and provide moral and spiritual guidance to their members. Ministers also help the sick and needy and supervise the religious educational programs of their church. Protestant ministers also have administrative duties in their congregations and may take on further responsibilities in their denomination at the regional or national level, or in community groups. Some Protestant ministers may also be involved in missionary work, teaching people around the world about their religion.

Protestant ministers are the spiritual leaders of their congregations. Their primary responsibility is leading worship services and preparing for those services. Most Protestant services include Bible readings, hymn singing, prayers, and a sermon written and delivered by the minister.

Protestant clergy also administer specific church rites, such as baptism, holy communion, and confirmation. They conduct weddings and funerals. Ministers advise couples concerning the vows and responsibilities of marriage. They may also act as marriage counselors for couples who are having marital difficulties. They visit the sick and comfort the bereaved.

Protestant ministers usually play an important part in the religious education of their congregations. They supervise Sunday school and similar Bible study programs and usually teach confirmation and adult education courses. The extent of their involvement in religious education programs and other church activities is often determined by the size of their congregations. In small churches, ministers may know most of the members personally and take an active role in everything that goes on. In larger churches, ministers may have to devote more time to administrative duties and delegate some of their other responsibilities.

Some ministers teach in seminaries and other schools. Others write for publications and give speeches within the Protestant community and to broader audiences. A growing number of ministers are employed only part-time and may serve more than one congregation or have a nonreligious part-time job.

Requirements

High School In high school, prospective Protestant ministers should study history and religion, plus English and speech to improve their teaching and speaking skills.

Music and fine arts classes will help strengthen their understanding and appreciation of the liturgy. Knowledge of a foreign language may help ministers better serve the needs of their congregations.

Postsecondary   While some denominations require that their ministers have little more than a high school education or Bible study, the majority of Protestant groups demand a bachelor's degree plus several years of specialized theological training. Study in these theological schools, of which there are about 150 in the United States and Canada, generally lasts about three years and leads to the degree of Master of Divinity.

Typically, prospective clergy receives their undergraduate degree in the liberal arts, although entrants come from a range of academic backgrounds. Course work should include English, foreign languages, philosophy, the natural sciences, psychology, history, social sciences, comparative religions, fine arts, and music.

Course work in seminary generally covers four areas: history, theology, the Bible, and practical ministry techniques. Practical ministry techniques include counseling, preaching, church administration, and religious education. In addition to classroom study and examinations, the seminary student serves at least one year as an intern to gain practical experience in leading services and other ministerial duties.

In general, the major Protestant denominations have their own training schools, but many of these schools admit students of other denominations. There are also several interdenominational colleges and theological schools that train the ministers. These students may receive additional training in the denomination in which they will be ordained.

Other Requirements Protestant ministers must meet the requirements of their individual denominations. Both men and women can become ordained ministers in most denominations today. Beyond formal requirements, Protestant ministers must possess a religious vocation—a strong feeling that God is calling them to the service of others through religious ministry. For most, this means giving material success a lower priority than spiritual matters.

Ministers need to be outgoing and friendly and have a strong desire to help others. They need to be able to get along with people from a wide variety of backgrounds. They need patience, sympathy, and open-mindedness to be able to listen to the problems of others, while maintaining a discreet and sincere respect. They need leadership abilities, including self-confidence, decisiveness, and the ability to supervise others. Ministers need to be aware that they will be relied on heavily by their congregation in times of trouble and stress, so it is important they keep the needs of their own families balanced with that of their congregations.

Exploring

The first step in exploring this career is to speak with your own minister about it. He or she can tell you more about it, help you discern your own calling, and put you in touch with other people and resources. It also makes sense to become as involved with your church as possible: teaching Sunday school, attending weekly services and Bible study, helping at other events. You might also want to volunteer with the sick or the elderly, particularly in institutions affiliated with your church.

Employers

Protestant ministers are usually employed by the congregations they serve. Most, but not all, congregations play a decisive role in selecting the person who will serve as their pastor. Some ministers may choose to work in seminaries, hospitals, or other church-run institutions. Other employment opportunities for clergy include social service work, such as counseling, youth work, family relations guidance, and teaching. Ministers may also find opportunities as chaplains in the armed forces, hospitals, mental health centers, prisons, and social agencies such as the YMCA.

Starting Out

Students should consult with their minister or contact the appropriate theological seminary to learn how to best meet entrance requirements. Some denominations do not require seminary training to become ordained. Smaller denominations may train part-time leaders, who eventually may seek ordination. Seminary graduates who cannot find ready employment may become directors of homes for the aged, the mentally handicapped, or orphans. Others may find employment in the social services, as missionaries, or in church-sponsored summer camps. Some ministers may take an unpaid position with a financially disadvantaged church in order to gain valuable experience.

Advancement

Newly ordained ministers generally begin their careers as pastors of small congregations or as assistant pastors in larger congregations. Advancement may take the form of getting a new or larger congregation of one's own. Protestant ministers may also advance into the hierarchy of their denominations. Many, though, do not seek advancement in the material sense, but find satisfaction in serving wherever they are most needed.

Work Environment

Ministers spend long hours working under a variety of conditions. There is no such thing as a standard workweek. They are very likely to have a set schedule of services, classes, and meetings, but ministers are on call at all times. They are called upon to visit the sick and the dying and to minister to the grieving at all hours. Protestant ministers may also be needed to fill in for colleagues who are away or otherwise unavailable—conducting services and meeting the pastoral needs of their colleagues' congregations.

Ministers in the mainstream Protestant denominations are well provided for—they usually have an office in the church building and a residence nearby. Such centrally located facilities make it easier to discharge their duties. It is the ministers' personal responsibility, however, to ensure that they strike the proper balance between work and family life.

Earnings

Salaries vary substantially for Protestant clergy depending on the individual's experience, the size of the congregation, its denomination, location, and financial status. The estimated average income of ministers is about $27,000 per year. Additional benefits usually include a housing stipend, which includes utilities, a monthly transportation allowance, health insurance, and other fringe benefits, which raise the average compensation for senior pastors in large congregations to over $50,000. Pension plans, travel stipends for research and rest, and grants for the education of their children are also included in many compensation packages. Clergy often are given money when they officiate at weddings and funerals. The minister sometimes donates this to the church or a charity. Some ministers of smaller congregations may add to their earnings by working at part-time nonreligious jobs.

Outlook
Currently, more than 400,000 Protestant ministers serve a variety of congregations in the United States. While overall membership in Protestant churches is growing, most of the mainline denominations, such as the Baptist, Lutheran, Methodist, and Presbyterian churches, are not. Aging membership has caused church budgets and membership to shrink, reducing the demand for full-time ministers. There has been a significant increase in nondenominational congregations. Overall, the increased cost of operating churches is expected to limit the demand for ministers. The closing or combining of smaller parishes, and the reduced availability of funds, has also lessened the need for full-time ministers. Although the number of ministry graduates is also declining, ministers should expect competition for some parish jobs, especially the more desirable, urban ones.

Demand for ministers will vary depending on the denomination, with nondenominational churches needing the most ministers. Graduates of theological schools have the best prospects for employment, as do ministers willing to work in rural churches with smaller congregations, salary, and benefits. They may also have to minister to two or more smaller congregations to earn a sufficient salary. Employment opportunities may depend on ministers retiring, passing away, or leaving the profession.

TO LEARN MORE ABOUT MINISTERS

Books

McPherson, Joyce. *The River of Grace: The Story of John Calvin.* Lebanon, Tenn.: Greenleaf Press, 1999.

Morgan, Nina. *Mother Teresa: Saint of the Poor.* Austin, Tex.: Raintree/Steck-Vaughn, 1998.

Severance, John B. *Gandhi: Great Soul.* New York: Houghton Mifflin, 1997.

Vernon, Louise A. *A Heart Strangely Warmed: The Life of John Wesley.* Lebanon, Tenn.: Greenleaf Press, 1994.

Wellman, Sam. *Billy Graham: The Great Evangelist.* Broomall, Penn.: Chelsea House, 1998.

Wellman, Sam. *T. D. Jakes.* Broomall, Penn.: Chelsea House, 2000.

Websites

Evangelical Lutheran Church in America (ELCA)
http://www.elca.org
For information about the national organization, including links to Lutheran seminaries

Presbyterian Church (USA)

http://www.pcusa.org
For information about the national organization, including links to Presbyterian seminaries

Southern Baptist Convention

http://www.sbc.net
For information about the national organization, including links to Baptist seminaries

Union Theological Seminary

http://www.uts.columbia.edu
An independent, nondenominational graduate school of theology whose mission is to educate men and women for ministries of the Christian faith and service in contemporary society

United Church of Christ

http://ucc.org
A church founded in 1957 as the union of several different Christian traditions

United Methodist Church

http://www.umc.org or *http://www.gbhem.org*
For information about the national organization, including links to Methodist seminaries

Where to Write

Besides your own pastor, you can consult the headquarters of your denomination for information about becoming a Protestant minister.

Evangelical Lutheran Church in America (ELCA)
8765 West Higgins Road
Chicago, IL 60631

Presbyterian Church (USA)
100 Witherspoon Street
Louisville, KY 40202

Southern Baptist Convention
901 Commerce
Nashville, TN 37203

United Methodist Church
Board of Higher Education and Ministry
PO Box 871
Nashville, TN 37202

TO LEARN MORE ABOUT MARTIN LUTHER KING JR.

Books

Davidson, Margaret. *I Have a Dream: The Story of Martin Luther King.* New York: Scholastic, 1991.

McKissack, Pat. *Martin Luther King Jr.: Man of Peace.* Springfield, N.J.: Enslow, 1991.

Patterson, Lillie. *Martin Luther King, Jr., and the Freedom Movement.* New York: Checkmark, 1993.

Peck, Ira. *The Life and Works of Martin Luther King Jr.* New York: Scholastic, 2000.

Stein R. Conrad. *The Asassination of Martin Luther King, Jr.* Danbury, Conn.: Children's Press, 1996.

Websites

Archer Audio Archives—Martin Luther King Jr.
http://www.archervalerie.com/mlk.html
An audio selection of King's speeches

CNN—Martin Luther King Jr. Day
http://cgi.cnn.com/SPECIALS/1998/mlk.page/
A collection of the 1998 national observances of King's birthday

Martin Luther King Jr.'s Assassination
http://home.stlnet.com/~cdstelzer/mlk.html
Questions posed by a St. Louis reporter about the details of King's death

Martin Luther King Jr. Tribute
http://www.lifemag.com/Life/mlk/mlk.html
A tribute from *Life* magazine, including pictures of Dr. King and excerpts from his writings

Interesting Places to Visit
Ebenezer Baptist Church
407 Auburn Avenue, N.E.
Atlanta, Georgia 30312
404/688-7263

The Martin Luther King Jr. Center for Nonviolent Social Change
449 Auburn Avenue, N.E.
Atlanta, Georgia 30312
404/524-1956

Martin Luther King Jr. National Historic Site
450 Auburn Avenue, N.E.
Atlanta, Georgia 30312-1525
404/331-5190 (24-hour recorded message)
404/331-6922

The National Civil Rights Museum
450 Mulberry Street (in the Lorraine Motel)
Memphis, Tennessee 38103-4214
901/521-9699

Schomberg Center for Research in Black Culture
515 Malcolm X Boulevard
New York, New York 10037-1801
212/491-2200

INDEX

Page numbers in *italics* indicate illustrations.

ABOUT THE AUTHOR

Brendan January graduated from Haverford College and Columbia University Graduate School of Journalism. He has written several nonfiction books for young readers, including one recognized as a Best Science Book of 1999 by the National Science Teachers Association. Brendan January is currently a journalist at the *Philadelphia Inquirer* and lives with his wife in New Jersey.